T0365854

AFRICAN STUDENTS
and *Their* DETERMINATION
for EDUCATION

AFRICAN STUDENT
AND EDUCATION

Ganiyu Jimoh

Archway Publishing books may be ordered through booksellers or by contacting:

Archway Publishing
1663 Liberty Drive
Bloomington, IN 47403
www.archwaypublishing.com
1 (888) 242-5904

Because of the dynamic nature of the Internet, any web addresses or links contained in this book may have changed since publication and may no longer be valid. The views expressed in this work are solely those of the author and do not necessarily reflect the views of the publisher, and the publisher hereby disclaims any responsibility for them.

Any people depicted in stock imagery provided by Thinkstock are models, and such images are being used for illustrative purposes only.
Certain stock imagery © Thinkstock.

ISBN: 978-1-4808-5403-1 (sc)
ISBN: 978-1-4808-5402-4 (e)

Print information available on the last page.

Archway Publishing rev. date: 11/27/2017

AFRICAN STUDENTS *and Their* DETERMINATION *for* EDUCATION

This is the story of Students in Africa and their everyday struggle to survive.

Author: Ganiyu Jimoh

Mr. Ganiyu Jimoh is a native of Owode Ketu in the western part of Nigeria. He grew up in a village in Owode and attended school in this village. His experience during this time prompted him to write this short story to show young school children that anything is possible if they put their mind to it. He has a bachelor from University of Phoenix and Masters from Loyola University New-Orleans, certificate from Cornel University. He is a veteran of the US Armed forces, Adjunct faculty at Upper Iowa University and a Captain with the Baton Rouge City Marshal/Constable office where he is the Chief of Operations. He is a member of Local State and Federal Task force. He is married to Lydia Jimoh and has five beautiful children.

This is the story of Students in a Nigerian village and their struggle to survive. We have chosen two brothers from a village called Igbogila in the western part of Nigeria, this story will illustrate how they survive daily in the phase of tremendous hardship, yet they do not complain but utilize the little they have to accomplish their daily task.

The two brothers are Lukuman and Fatai. They are six and seven years old. Lukumon and Fatai are member of a large family, they have nine brothers and sisters, their parents are farmers and they live in the middle of African jungle where the sound of lion and elephant is part of daily life. Their parents struggle to provide for the family, they depend on what they plant and hunt for food, normal amenities that we take for granted in the Western World are nonexistence in this family.

The family lives in a self-built house that sometimes takes years to complete.

Their daily routine begins with Lukumon and Fatai helping their father to cultivate his farm where he grows needed food for the family. Normal routine begins at 05:00 am. They begin by walking three miles to the farm and picking up food to bring home to their mother. At 07:00 am they begin their journey to school, on their way they stop at the village café to eat a bowl of rice and some vegetables, this café provides good nourishment to this student before going in to a long day of schooling, the breakfast is 10c. They are also joined by their fellow students at the café.

All students wore the same uniform, some parents are able to provide a pair of slippers for their kids while some parents do without, Lukumon and Fatai parents are one of those that could not afford the expense so they do without, but that never stopped them from making the two mile walk from home to school every day. They enjoyed going to school every day and they are straight "A" students.

Arriving at school before 08:00 am begins with a prayer that all students and teachers participate, followed by the singing of the Nigerian national anthem, any kids caught skipping these activities are severely punished by the principal.

By 08:00 am every students are expected in the class rooms where the teachers are waiting. The class begins with a brief encouraging word, such as how hard everyone will work to accomplish their goals and the expectation of their teacher and parents.

English, Mathematics, Biology, Chemistry, Physics, History and Geography are some of the subjects taught daily in Lukumon and Fatai's School.

Every student is expected to participate in the classroom. Activities include the teacher calling on each student and making sure they ask or answer questions during class. Part of the routine is taking quizzes at end of the lesson to gauge what the student have learned.

During one of the class instructions the teacher noticed Lukumon isn't paying attention and seems withdrawn, he called him to his desk to find out what was wrong. Lukumon stated that a student named Dayo took his lunch money preventing him from purchasing breakfast or lunch for the next few days and he also threatened him by stating that he will beat him if he tells anyone about their encounter.

The teacher immediately summoned Dayo to his classroom, he forced him to return the money taken, and was also disciplined for his behavior. Dayo's parents were also informed about his behaviors, and he was also disciplined by his father.

Some of the daily rules enforced by the school system include:

No weapon such as knife or any sharp object in school. Since no one is allowed to own a gun except law enforcement officers, no student or teacher has such a weapon.

No fighting is allowed.

No stealing or bullying is permitted in school

Late comers are severely punished.

Class rules include:

No talking in class unless authorize by the teacher

Students must raise their hands before responding to a question or comments.

Any student violating these rules will be punished. The punishment may include having the student stand in a corner with their hands raised over their head for 30 minutes, or receiving some lashes on their backside carried out by the teacher or the principal.

Lunch

Students form a straight line in front of their dining hall to eat lunch. Their lunch consists of rice, beans, and some meat depending on the day of the week. Lukumon and Fatai always look forward to these meals because this is the only balance meal they have for the day.

Physical Activities

Students are allowed 2 hours of physical activities that include track, sack race, soccer, and basketball. The student looks forward to these activities daily because this is the only real break they have from classroom instruction.

End of School Day

The school starts 0700 am and ends by 4pm, Lukumon and Fatai makes the three mile journey back to their village. School is all year around except for Christmas, New Year and Independence Day. On their way home they sometimes encounter deer, snakes, and few other small creatures, but this does not bother them because this is part of the village norm in most African countries

Upon arriving home Lukumon and Fatai quickly change in to their work clothes and leave to join their parents in the jungle by the cocoa farm where they help to cultivate the cocoa seeds. These seeds are used to produce coffee. The coffee traders periodically visit the village to purchase some of this seeds. The family uses the money to buy their children school uniform, books, and school supplies. They also assist in hunting wild game for the family consumption. A good hunting day involves successful hunting of antelopes, and other big animals. During hunting season they always come across dangerous animals such as Lions, Tigers, Hyenas, and poisonous snakes. The family always eat from the same bowl and eat together as a family. They look out for each other, they protect each other, and always render help to family members and others. The family always shares their food with other people from the village including wild game.

Rainy season bring many challenges. The roofs to their residence leaks because it is made of bamboo, they always have to find an area of the house that does not have so much leak.

Lukumon and Fatai graduated from high school with a 4.0 GPA. In the face of the hardships they were able to make it through with flying colors. The two brothers received a four year scholarship from their State University to study agriculture.

Four years later they graduated from college and came back home to help other young children in their village, by helping them to succeed.

Some of the assistance include purchasing text books, clothing, shoes, and creating a breakfast and lunch program. They established a nonprofit organization in which they solicit company donation to cover expense for this program. They also help local clinics in obtaining medication such as aspirin, Tylenol, and minor medicine for children and the elders. They place a lot of emphasis on annual vaccinations for the children to prevent cholera, typhus, malaria and other diseases.

The latest project is assisting the villagers in building brick houses for their family. The two brothers also built a three bedroom solid concrete home for their mother and father. They are now responsible for making sure the rest of their brothers and sisters receive adequate education.

Lukumon and Fatai's uncle is the local Chief for the village. His responsibility includes making sure each villagers follow the law, and the fair sharing of food among villagers, helping with fixing the roads and providing the means for clean water and the wellbeing of all villagers.

Lukumon and Fatai's sister preparing Gari for the whole family, this Gari is part of the meal consumed by the family daily.

The Gari product is transformed to Eba which is consumed in the form of FUFU and can also be in the form of drink such as drinking a cereal.

Lukumon and Fatai's parents and grandparents welcoming visitors to the village.

Uncle Jimoh' s mother, his great uncle and member of the family gathered together to celebrate his arrival since this was the first time they've seen him in 15 years. His family were very surprised because they were not expecting him.

Member of Lukumon and Fatai's family receiving family members from the United States of America.

Uncle Jimoh, his sister, and brothers travelled almost 100 miles to the village where he was born to visit family members. The villagers were so excited to see him, some did not even recognize him since it has been so long since they saw him. He was a young boy when he left but came back as a grown man.

Mobee Royal Slave Relic in Badagry, great source of information about the history of slavery in Africa.

This relic is the location of one of the Slave trade in Africa especially Nigeria. Half a mile from its location is the entrance to where slaves walked through before being placed on the ships to foreign locations.

Lukumon's family member conducting a prayer vigil in the village of Owode in Ogun State. Uncle Jimoh and member of the family during his visit to the village.

Prayer is a strong tradition among family members, you never do anything without praying, and this prayer is led by the elders.

Picture below is Lukumon uncle who is the chief in the village. Uncle Jimoh and his friend from the United States are visiting the Nigerian village. His friend was so thrilled and amazed that he has made three trips on his own back to Nigeria.

The chief is look upon as a spiritual leader who people goes to for advice or help.

Mr. Constant Payne and uncle Jimoh are holding the coronation stick and the crown of the chief. Mr. Constant was extremely happy because this is the first time he has ever travelled out of the US and meeting the Chief is an icing on the cake.

The first lady, who happen to be the wife of the chief, was also present, she was very excited to receive the visitors.

Picture of some Nigerian artifact, each carries a significant meaning.

The statue in the pictures signifies different events or history. If you look carefully you can see the statues of kings, villagers carrying water on their heads, farmers sitting down relaxing, and women in traditional costumes.

Michael Otedola College of primary education is a School where teachers are being trained to be elementary and middle school teachers.

The training school in any given year accommodates at least a 1000 students who later become teachers and principals of local and state schools.

A meeting of engineers, political person and business man in a fried chicken restaurant.

The conversation involved how funds can be raised for some of the nonprofit organizations and providing scholarships for some of the students from the villages.

A street in Agege Lagos State and the picture of buses and mopeds used as transportation by the public.

Uncle Jimoh and Mr. Constant his friend meeting with his uncle who happens to be a senator in Nigeria.

Picture of one of the popular shopping mall in Lagos. This is one of the busiest Malls in ILeki Nigeria.

Cars driving through the jungle sometimes for miles before reaching their destination.

To get to some of the villages from the city, you have to drive hundreds of mile before reaching your destination, and sometimes you will have to drive through the jungle. If you travel early you might be fortunate to see different animals crossing the roads. You will see animals such as Lions, Hyenas, and others crossing from one side of the jungle to the other.

A Mother traveling through the main road, returning from the family farm.

A woman from the village returning from the farm, carrying some food materials on her head. Women participate in farm work just as men do, they transport the food home by carrying them on their heads.

Picture of the local church.

A picture of the main church in the village where villagers worship. Lukumon and Fatai parents attend prayer service every Sunday and bible studies on Wednesday.

Picture of Mr. Constant and Uncle Jimoh with his Mom. his great aunt, and his nephew in law.

One of the major ports in Lagos.

Most of the ships coming to Lagos Nigeria dock at this port. At any given time you might see at least 100-150 ships from different countries at the pier. They either stop to deliver or pick up goods.

Picture of Mr. Jimoh and his family sitting under the tree with 107 year old uncle, sharing some old war stories, growth, loss trials and tribulations.

Picture of one of the Kings Palaces in Lagos, Nigeria.

This palace houses the king and his family, and visitation is by invitation only.

Picture of Mr. Jimoh and his uncle who is the Chief in the village. He is responsible for the well-being of the 7200 residents who live in the village.

Pictures of Elementary, middle and high school students on their way to school, briefly stopping to eat breakfast at the village café.

Uncle Jimoh and Mr. Constant treated the school children to a free breakfast, Lukumon and Fatai are some of the kids in the group.

Picture of Mr. Jimoh at the river in Badagry, Ogun State. This river has a significant meaning, it is the main route for slave trade in Nigeria. Fishermen uses the river to fish. Their survival depends on the amount of fish caught daily, especially since some of the fish is consumed by them and their family and the rest taken to the market for sale.

This is the main river slave ships travelled through after picking up their cargo from Nigeria to transport to different countries and continents.

Uncle Jimoh, his aunt, his uncle, his mother, Mr. Constant and nephew in law in front of the community center and home for orphans.

Pictures of Elementary School, Middle School and High School.

There are five parallel buildings similar to the building in this picture, this facility houses elementary, middle and high school.

Picture of Mr. Jimoh's family members and people from the village.

Here is a picture of Uncle Jimoh and his aunt who happens to be the only medical doctor in the village.

Picture below is uncle Jimoh and his sister Ms. Shadia Jimoh and Mr. constant Payne. Ms. Shadia is a school teacher in one of the local high school in Lagos Nigeria. She is also an entrepreneur who owns a grocery store, and her daily routine involved training our nieces and nephews about responsibility. She involved them in the operation of the Store. The store opens by 06:00 am and maintained by employees. The children assist in opening the store before they proceed to school, and they return to the store to assist in the operation of the store until closing. Some of their responsibilities includes monitoring the cash register, greeting customers and stacking the shelves. Everyone in the family sends their children to Ms. Shadia for some training.

Ms. Shadiat is the mother of Mr. Dayo Akanni who is one of the owners of Dovewell Group Company in Nigeria. This company sells oil supplies and equipment to major oil companies like Exxon-Mobil, Texaco, Shell and others.

Uncle Jimoh and his military buddy Mr. Constant Payne standing behind one of Mr. Dayo's vehicle in his compound at ILeki Lagos Nigeria. Typical house in Nigeria owned by middle class families usually contain 5-6 bedrooms minimum, and might be two or three stories high. Given the difference in currency the price of building a good homes in Nigeria is cheaper than most American or European homes.

Dressing comfortably is part of Nigerian Culture, there so many types of clothing in Nigeria, you can dress in your traditional robe or European attire.

Captain Ganiyu Jimoh is the Chief of Operation with the Baton Rouge City Constable's Office. Captain Jimoh supervises 5 divisions of the Constable office. He is also the training director for the Agency, he created the first Reserve Academy for the Constables office.

He is a member of the Local State, and Federal Task force, and member of National Organization of Black Law Enforcement.

He is active member of the Egbe Omo Yoruba Baton Rouge chapter, and the United Nigerian Organization in Baton Rouge, La.

Languages.

These are some of the languages spoken in Nigeria.

English is Nigeria official language that everyone speaks, some speak Pidgin English which is a form of easy casual communication among family and friends.

Yoruba: - spoken by the Yoruba people in Western part of Nigeria, city such as Oyo, Ogun, Ondo, Osun Kwara, Kogi and Lagos State.

Hausa: - Most of the population associated with this language are Muslims from the Northern part of Nigeria. People from Kano, Kaduna, Katsina, and Bauchi Jigawa speaks Hausa.

Igbo:-Spoken by people from Anambra, Ebony, Enugu, Aniocha, and most of the Eastern part of Nigeria.

Special Thanks to my Wife

My wife Lydia Jimoh and I met 25 years ago when I was a young entrepreneur trying to run a small business, I remember how we went door to door trying to solicit business. We did not mind the door being slammed in our faces we persevered, we were able to build the business to where we were comfortable enough to start a family. Lydia was my secretary and office manager at the same time she never complained or worried about any issue that we faced, I learned a lot from her.

Lydia and I have been together for over 22years, we have five beautiful girls. Without her I will not be able to do what I do, her support and word of encouragement is what kept me going every day. I never thought I will find such a woman of peace and tranquility, her demeanor and personality has no match, nothing phases her, she is my backbone, my best friend and the love of my life. I thank her for all the support she has given me over the years and I love her very much.

I would also like to thank my Boss, Constable Reginald Brown Sr., without him I would not have the opportunity to be part of the Constable organization, he saw me as a qualified individual who fit in to his organization very well, he did not worry about my ethnic background or what country I came from. He gave me the same opportunity that he gave everyone else. This man is my mentor and role model. He taught me how to be humble and be respectful to everyone, and his leadership skills are the best I have ever seen. He was a Major with the East Baton Rouge Sheriff's office before running for the Constable position. He was the State president of the Louisiana City Marshal and Constable Association. The architect of the Gun Safety Program in Louisiana and the host of a radio program called "Major Topics" in Baton Rouge Louisiana. He is married to Mrs. Gayle Boyd Brown. He is the recipient of 1997 Golden Deeds Award in Baton Rouge for his contribution to the community. He is known as father of law enforcement in Baton Rouge.

I also extends my gratitude to Chief Ray Antoine, the Chief Deputy, who has been instrumental in guiding me. He is also a retired Captain from East Baton Rouge Sheriff's office.

Thanks to Ms. Wanda Thomas and all my fellow employees.

Thanks to my Father–in-law Anthony Lawrence who has been responsible for helping me in learning about law enforcement, especially as the City Prosecutor, his experience has been beneficial to me. Also my mother-in-Law Claire Lawrence and the rest of the family for their support.

Author Remarks

The author draws on his experience as a young child growing up in Africa. Experiencing the same hardship endure by Lukumon and Fatai and others from Africa.

The lesson to children of the World is that you should not be deter from your dreams by any obstacle. If student from this third world country can get educated in the face of a mounting obstacles, no child in the democratic world should go without adequate education especially since resources are abundant and available to every children and adult.

Remember " education is your Lifeline" since not all of us can be a professional football player, pro basketball player, a movie star, and a professional singer, all we have at the end is the education that is provided to us.

Remember to be part of the solution to bullying, we must make this epidemic a thing of the past.

Let's treat everyone with respect and dignity, and be respectful to everybody including your teacher and parents.

Study hard, listen to your parents and be yourself.

Printed in the United States
by Baker & Taylor Publisher Services